The Expat Activity Book
20 Personal Development Exercises for Gaining Insight and Maximizing Your Potential Wherever You Are

Jodi Harris, MSW

World Tree Coaching
www.worldtreecoaching.com

World Tree Coaching
www.worldtreecoaching.com

About This Book

For more than ten years I've worked with individuals who are confronting the challenges of staying true to themselves while living outside of their home cultures. Whether you're a chronic expat, a study abroad student, a recently returned volunteer or intern, or an immigrant, it's incredibly easy to lose sight of who you are when everything is constantly changing around you.

These exercises are the outcome of years of direct practice and personal experience (I've been living or traveling abroad for over fifteen years). They are not designed to help you "get abroad" or "reboot your life" (although that very well might be the outcome). They are simply designed to help you home in on what matters to you…wherever you are. And, they do that, while taking into account all of the many, many challenges and gifts that a worldwide existence offers. They focus on the here and now, with an eye out for what's next.

How to Complete the Activities

Great news! What you do with these activities is completely up to you. Every activity is self-paced and designed with maximum flexibility in mind. Each exercise includes information on a recommended "best time" to do the work, but I invite you to consider this a suggestion. There's no wrong way to work through this program. All of the activities can be revisited from time to time. In short – this is a fluid program that is designed to be flexible and grow with you. You set the agenda.

Disclaimer

I believe these activities are an incredible resource for helping individuals gain insight, reignite passion and pursue new learning while experiencing the joys of international travel or learning. They are meant to be used as a guide. While I thoroughly believe you will find numerous positive benefits from completing this program, the activities herein should not be used in lieu of professional advice. It is recommended and assumed that anyone completing these activities will consult with the appropriate legal, medical, financial, business and/or spiritual professional as needed while undertaking these activities. All of the activities are designed to be completed by adults. All decisions made, actions taken and outcomes experienced by any individual completing these activities are understood to be exclusively his/hers alone and are not the responsibility of World Tree Coaching or Jodi Harris, MSW.

Copyright and Use

All of the content provided here is copyrighted and the property of World Tree Coaching. The content here should not be distributed, reproduced or altered without the permission of World Tree Coaching or its representative (Jodi Harris). Please contact Jodi@worldtreecoaching.com with any questions or to learn more about how to purchase copies. More information about World Tree Coaching can be found at: www.worldtreecoaching.com.

World Tree Coaching

My Story

First things first I guess – I'm a world traveler. I've lived in Spain, Japan, Northern Ireland, the Dominican Republic and Madagascar. I've traveled in dozens of countries over five continents. Frankly, if you're reading this, you probably have too...or at least you imagine you will have before too long.

These experiences don't define me, but they do play significant backdrop to the other aspects of my life. I grew up in a small town in Central Texas fantasizing about the great big world and never really imagined I'd stay in one place for long. But, the road wasn't always clear-cut. I found it easy to decide to study abroad in Spain as an undergraduate and then taught English with the JET Progam in Japan right after college. But, after spending a couple of years teaching high school, I felt called to make a shift and eventually decided to pursue a Masters Degree in Social Work. Because of my Spanish language skills and background as a teacher, I was quickly identified to work with immigrant students. And, my interest in conflict resolution landed me an internship in Belfast, Northern Ireland where I worked with Catholic and Protestant trauma survivors at a local community center. Upon completion of my MSW, I returned to Austin where I worked for four years at a local health center providing counseling and support services (mostly to Spanish-speaking immigrants) while completing my clinical hours and eventually acquiring my LCSW.

My husband and I met during my senior year at the University of Texas. We were mutually ecstatic to find someone who shared our interest in travel. We committed ourselves to going abroad and at times even found that this meant that we were temporarily separated. Eventually, however, the desire to have a family and create a sense of home won out and we knew that the only way to keep up our nomadic life was to find a way to do it and become part of a community.

The year after our second child was born, my husband took a position as a Foreign Service Officer with the US Department of State. For me this meant, once again, the ability to adapt my interests and passions to encompass a worldwide view. The only problem was, I was really at a loss for what those had become. I remember one day crying in the car to my husband, "I have a masters degree and all I do is bake bread!" I struggled for months with the challenges of finding what exactly I wanted to do with myself. Eventually, mostly through serendipity, I applied for and accepted an offer for my dream job. I went to work as a program coordinator for Peace Corps Dominican Republic supervising and training social work Peace Crops volunteers. I loved it...and then, overworked and stressed out, I crashed...and then I found out I was pregnant...and then we packed up and moved. Every part of me was thinking, "What am I doing!?"

Our third child was born after our departure from the Dominican Republic and it was then that I started to step back and examine more fully all of these interests and skill sets adding one on top of the other. I felt incredibly anchorless. For the first time, I realized that this wasn't just a series of adventures, but my life – my real, actual, no-going-back life. I knew that somewhere in the midst of all of this was the real me, but so much time adapting to new things made me feel like I couldn't find who that person really was. My past experience with things like this was to start flailing around for answers, but this time I just decided to slow down, to stop, to immerse myself in creating awareness of what I felt drawn to and what didn't change (even when everything else was shifting). Through that examination, I began to be more aware of my values and what I really wanted out of life. I stopped seeing myself as wishy-washy and undecided and began to see the trends in my past experiences and interests. I got bold about what I love (family, friends, parties, food, books, exercise, nature) and started doing away with the things that didn't uplift me (owning stuff, attending events or meetings in which I have no interest, doing too many things).

Through that process I decided to begin training as a coach. I now run my own life coaching business – World Tree Coaching. I've turned the thousands of hours I've spent over the years receiving the stories of people living outside their home cultures into my dream job. I absolutely love what I do and the people I work with. And, I'm infinitely grateful to be able to share this adventure with my wonderful husband and my smart, funny and just-plain-awesome children. My personal journey, like yours, has had its ups and downs, but I'd not have it any other way.

As expats, our challenges are not unlike those of our peers who stay in one place. We're all trying to get it right, to live out our dreams, to build a foundation of clarity and presence and, ultimately I think, happiness. But, here's the big difference: we do it all while the rules around us are changing. It's just so easy to get lost out there. Not one of us should be alone in trying to figure it out. I love, love, love working with people who want to weather change with their hearts and minds intact. My hope is that this book will be one small piece in helping you get there. I hope you enjoy it!

With love,

Jodi

World Tree Coaching

World Tree Coaching
www.worldtreecoaching.com

Contents

Activity One: The Hello Checklist

Activity Two: Visualizing Your Adventure

Activity Three: Priorities

Activity Four: The Un-Busy To Do List

Activity Five: Be Curious

Activity Six: In The Comfort Zone

Activity Seven: Journaling Culture Shock

Activity Eight: Balancing You

Activity Nine: Community

Activity Ten: Lost and Found

Activity Eleven: Taking Credit for New Skills

Activity Twelve: Your Life Story

Activity Thirteen: The Space Box

Activity Fourteen: Life's Little Go-Bag

Activity Fifteen: 20 Questions for Getting Unstuck

Activity Sixteen: Bad Day Permission Slip

Activity Seventeen: Your Life Vision

Activity Eighteen: Dressing for What's Next

Activity Nineteen: On Thoughts and Emotions

Activity Twenty: The Goodbye Checklist

Activity One: The Hello Checklist

Purpose:

This exercise will help you prioritize your "must-dos" before and during the arrival phase of transition.

Introduction:

You've arrived, or you're about to! There's just so much to see and so many things to do and all those people to meet! It can be really overwhelming. You'll be bombarded with people telling you the long list of must-dos that will help you feel settled and at home. But, only you can know what you need to feel settled. One person's must-dos might be your put-off-until-tomorrows.

Instructions:

Use the chart below to make a checklist of the things that are the most important to you mentally and emotionally during the settling in process. Focus in on the keys to your overall well-being. Take some time before you leave to create the list – because there will be plenty of potential distractions and interruptions once you arrive. Once you're ready to check-off one of your "Must-Dos" – simply do so in the "Done" space. If you need more spaces, you can always add these on a blank sheet of paper or in a journal or planner.

My Must Dos	Done
Ex. *Find out where to buy good cheese.*	✓
Ex. *Set up my music system so my house doesn't feel so quiet.*	✓

World Tree Coaching
www.worldtreecoaching.com

Activity Two: Visualizing Your Adventure

Purpose:

This activity is designed to prepare you for what will and will not happen during your time abroad. It's a fantastic thing to do in the months, weeks or days leading up to a big transition, trip or vacation, but you'll definitely come back to it periodically for the great reminders it provides.

Introduction:

Any time we have something new laid out before us, we begin the process of creating our biggest hopes and greatest fears. There is something to be gained from the pull we feel in each direction. The key is finding a way to bring these up as a means of growth, without holding so tightly on to them that we lose sight of what is actually happening around us. NOTE: This is a visualization exercise. While most people find visualization helps them come face to face with both hopes and fears, for others it can bring up past worries and even trauma. Seek the help of a professional as needed if your reactions to the exercise cause significant stress, anxiety or other adverse reactions.

Instructions:

(1) Find a place where you can collect your thoughts. A place where you can be alone with what's going on in your head is best. Begin to bring to mind the images you've created about what your next journey is going to be like. What will the sounds be, the smells, the people, your house or lodging? What conversations will you have? What people will you meet? Allow yourself to completely give in to your wildest fantasies of what this adventure will be like. Include both your dreams of perfection and your fears of challenge. Be bold! These are just thoughts and daydreams. Own them. Don't judge. You don't have to wallow in them, but get up close and personal. Take time to really view what you're creating in your mind in all facets. Write those images in the space provided here (or on your own paper or journal):

_____
_____
_____
_____
_____
_____
_____
_____
_____
_____
_____
_____
_____
_____
_____
_____

(2) Go back and read over what you've written. Read it again. And again.

(3) Next, tell yourself this: "Some of this will happen. Some of it will not." Say it again.

(4) Finally, close your eyes. Allow the mental image you've created to come into view – both the things that are likely to happen and the things that are not likely to happen. Bring up the beautiful fantasies and the worrisome difficulties. And now, visualize this paper with your images written down, being folded up, packaged up, neatly tied and sealed. Imagine it nesting down somewhere you carry with you – your heart, your mind or even your suitcase. And now, as you begin your journey some of these images will become reality. And, of course, many will not. When you find you encounter snippets of your mental image here and there – think of your list, wrapped up and waiting, bits and pieces of it being revealed each and every day.

Activity Three: Priorities

Purpose:

This activity is designed to help you more clearly formulate goals and priorities during transition.

Introduction:

A trip or a move abroad can be an excellent opportunity to set a few new priorities for your life. It's a great time to tap into what really matters and examine your values.

Focusing in on specific priorities is a bit like setting goals. But, there's one big difference – and it's a good one! When we set goals, we're focusing on specific things that we want to achieve or get out of a given situation. The only problem is when you're going abroad everything is about to change. So, unfortunately, you might find yourself throwing all of those best-laid plans right out the window. Turning goals into priorities might just seem like semantics, but it really can be a way to gain flexibility and cultivate success.

This activity will help you home in on what you're really saying when you set goals for your international adventures. When you really listen to what matters (and what your goals say about you), then you're setting a nice list of priorities.

Instructions:

1) List your top 3 "goals" for your trip abroad. Here are some examples to give you an idea: become fluent in the local language, learn about the local culture, eat great food, make new friends, see the sights. You may have more than 3 goals in mind, but try to focus on the top 3 here. If you need more space, you can always add lines or use a separate piece of paper or your journal.

1.
2.
3.

2) Brainstorm values that each of those goals might represent. For example, if becoming fluent in the local language is one of your goals, perhaps the values that represents for you are love of learning, need for connection, or security. For each goal, write down a few possible values.

	Goal 1	Goal 2	Goal 3
Values			
Values			
Values			
Values			

3) Now go back and look at your goals again. Do they seem clearer now? Let's take our example goal again – *Become fluent in the local language*. Let's say you decided that your desire to become fluent in the local language partially relates to your love of learning, but also represents your need for security (another way of saying, "I need to feel safe and understood."). You've learned something about yourself and why that goal is so important. So, now it's easier to set some priorities around that goal. Here are a few examples:

- Learn the vocabulary I need to ask for help, directions and instructions.
- Meet people I can practice with, but who can also tell me more about making my way in this new culture.
- Gain enough language skills to read the local newspaper – this will help with language, but also keep me informed about what's happening in my new community.
- Meet other expats and spend time learning about their experiences.
- Read up on the region's history, culture and people.

So you see, the priorities you set here are a list of options. Some of them you might check off easily, but others you'll revisit time and again – because they're about your lifestyle, not boxes on a page. The exciting thing is that the list of priorities are open and flexible – any time you do anything listed here – your can remind yourself, "This is the way I 'learn the local language'." You free yourself up to fulfill your goals in a variety of ways.

Do this for each of your goals below. You have 8 priority boxes on the next page, fill in as many as you like. You can always go back and add more (or even attach an additional sheet or recreate this chart in a journal or planner).

	Goal 1	Goal 2	Goal 3
Values			
Priorities			
Priorities			
Priorities			
Priorities			
Priorities			
Priorities			
Priorities			
Priorities			

World Tree Coaching
www.worldtreecoaching.com

Activity Four: The Un-Busy To Do List

Purpose:

With this exercise you will start to tackle your to-do list in a whole new way. This is about simplifying your crazy life so you can live more by doing less. Feeling overwhelmed? Then it's time to get un-busy! This exercise is a dream come true for those times when you're preparing for a move.

Introduction:

We live in a world where being busy is considered a sign of productivity and success. And yet, most people (all people?) would prefer to be less busy. Most of us would value a full life (a life of a wide array of activities we truly love) over a mish-mash of random stuff we feel compelled to do, but from which we gain very little pleasure.

The challenge that expats face in this area is that each move is filled with the type of busy-ness that most people only really have to experience a couple of times in their lives. Relocation, job change, a whole new set of friends – many of us do this repeatedly, year after year…for decades!

As a result, it's not enough for us just to conquer busy-ness with new strategies for focusing in on what we most need to do and most enjoy, we have to do this while actually getting things done. I mean, those bags aren't going to pack themselves!

So here's your chance to sort through all the muck on that to-do list, get things done and toss out all those extras that are cluttering up your time.

Instructions:

1) Use the To-Do List below (it continues on the following page for the super-busy people out there) to write down everything on your to-do list. Don't hold back. Include everything here – things you've committed to, things you're vaguely committed to, things you "should" do, the things you'd most like to do.

My To Do List

World Tree Coaching
www.worldtreecoaching.com

2) Now, you're going to start working on making that to-do list a bit more manageable. So, the next step is to define your to-do list categories. Spaces are provided below. The categories included here are: Must-Do, Would Like To Do and Do Not Need To Do. It's up to you to define them. Here are some examples of how you might do that:

Must-Do: *If I don't do this then we will have a major problem on our hands.*

Would Like To Do: *These things can wait, but doing them would bring me or someone I love much joy. My life would feel fuller with the things on this list.*

Do Not Need To Do: *Simply put, I do not NEED to do these things. I might feel compelled to do them, or pressure, or if I don't do them I will feel like people are looking down on me, but I do not actually NEED to do them.*

My Definitions

Must-Do:

Would Like To Do:

Do Not Need To Do:

3) Now it's time to get rid of some of that to-do list clutter. There's no time like the present to toss some stuff off that list and designate it to the Do Not Need To Do category. So, use the space on the next page to start sorting. A couple of examples are listed below to help you get started.

MUST-DO	WOULD LIKE TO DO	DO NOT NEED TO DO
Apply for visas	Shop for cool local souvenirs to take home for friends	Make cupcakes for my kids' end-of-year party.
Have a date-night with my husband at our favorite restaurant - after all, we may not ever get to eat there again.	Throw a brunch to say goodbye to my girlfriends in the neighborhood.	Attend a happy hour for my husband's colleague.

My Un-Busy To Do List

MUST-DO	WOULD LIKE TO DO	DO NOT NEED TO DO

4) The final step to this activity is figuring out how you're going to put this into action. And that is entirely up to you. There may be things from your DO NOT NEED TO DO LIST that you find creeping into your daily activities. The most important thing here is that you're aware of that happening. This is about being mindful of what you're doing while you're doing it. And, there's no need to judge yourself when that happens. We're all human and from time to time it can be really challenging to sort through so many competing priorities. But now that you have a greater awareness of where all of these to-dos fit, you have a much better chance of really sticking to the things that matter most.

World Tree Coaching
www.worldtreecoaching.com

World Tree Coaching

Activity Five: Be Curious

Purpose:

This exercise is designed to help you own up to your inner explorer without the cumbersome judgments we often place on being curious. It is ideally started before you begin a major transition, but it can be updated as you go along. It is an ongoing activity to be undertaken throughout your journey.

Introduction:

No matter where you are on your big adventure, you undoubtedly have hundreds of questions - from the practical (Do I need a visa for that?) to the somewhat mundane (How early will I be able to get my cup of coffee?).

Unfortunately, most of us learn early in life that asking too many questions is not okay. In fact, we often stifle our curiosity out of concerns for looking stupid, naïve or annoying. But, the truth is you *are* curious! You're an adventurer! You're a seeker of new and interesting things.

Instructions:

Use this space to write down the questions that you have. There's space here for 34 questions, but you can challenge yourself to come up with even more questions about your transition, the place you'll be going and the life you might have there. These can be questions about you, the world around you, your loved ones – anything! They can be short-term or long-term questions. If you like, you can assign the questions a category in the middle column (e.g. personal, professional, practical, cultural, etc). Then, use the check boxes at the right to mark off when you encounter a response that satisfies you.

Note that you're not checking off "answers." The most important thing to note about this exercise is that not every question has an answer. A lifestyle of adventure has a lot of ambiguity. Rarely, are things exactly as they seem. So, focus in on what satisfies you as a response to the questions you list. If you get a clear-cut answer – fantastic! If you don't, well that's just fine too.

QUESTION	CATEGORY	SATISFACTION
1.		
2.		
3.		
4.		

World Tree Coaching
www.worldtreecoaching.com

5.		
6.		
7.		
8.		
9.		
10.		
11.		
12.		
13.		
14.		
15.		
16.		
17.		
18.		
19.		

20.		
21.		
22.		
23.		
24.		
25.		
26.		
27.		
28.		
29.		
30.		
31.		
32.		
33.		
34.		

World Tree Coaching

Activity Six: In the Comfort Zone

Purpose:

The goal of this activity is to help create deeper awareness regarding the times when you're taking on experiences outside your comfort zone. While this activity is one that you can do any time you're traveling (especially during times when you're feeling stretched thin), it's best done at the very beginning of your time in a new place.

Introduction:

If you're a world traveler (or an aspiring one), the saying really is true – "Life begins at the end of your comfort zone." However, no one out there is going to say that pushing the limits of your comfort zone is a walk in the park. In fact, even when you enjoy stretching yourself to you outer limits – it's exhausting! Anyone who has spent time traveling understands how much more tiring it is to spend a day surrounded by languages, customs, people and foods that are new to you.

Developing a deeper more mindful awareness of the times when you're outside your comfort zone can be key to successfully navigating transition. The point of this exercise is not to place judgment on the times when you felt the most challenged or the most at ease. It's simply to help you raise consciousness around the fact that you are definitely experiencing things that are new, strange and sometimes even scary. The reflection section in particular can provide insight into handling stressful situations as they occur in the future.

Instructions:

1) Choose a time frame in which you'd like to plot your experiences on the comfort zone scale. A one-day timeframe can be doable, but you can also decide to plot your feelings off and on over the course of a week, a month or even a year.

2) This exercise uses the following scale for plotting your comfort zone: Rate your experience from 1-10, with 1 being 100% within your comfort zone and 10 being as far outside your comfort zone as you can imagine. Record the information in the chart on the next page. Five spaces are provided in the following pages, but additional experiences can be recorded on blank paper or in a journal. An example is shown here.

Date
April 21, 2014
Experience (who, what, where, etc.)
I attended an opening event for my spouse's work. I found myself having to meet tons of people I barely knew and most of the time it was very difficult to communicate. I thought my language skills in the host country language were great, but when asked to talk about interesting topics, I completely drew a blank.

Where were you on the comfort zone scale? 6
What feelings came up for you at this place on the scale?
Feelings of inadequacy. I felt like I had nothing to offer. I felt like "the trailing spouse." I was frustrated because sometimes I really thought I had something to contribute, but just couldn't make it happen. I did meet some new people who seemed nice – that made me feel a little happy...or hopeful.
What reflections, thoughts or insight did you gain from this experience?
I think I need a buddy in situations like this. I might see if in the future I could bring a friend. Or, perhaps I will try to find out who some of these people are and really try to spend my time talking with the ones with whom I feel I can communicate. I realize too that being seen as more than a trailing spouse is really important to me. Perhaps this means I need to do some networking and look into opportunities to do things professionally that represent me.

Date
Experience (who, what, where, etc.)
Where were you on the comfort zone scale?
What feelings came up for you at this place on the scale?
What reflections, thoughts or insight did you gain from this experience?

Date
Experience (who, what, where, etc.)
Where were you on the comfort zone scale?
What feelings came up for you at this place on the scale?
What reflections, thoughts or insight did you gain from this experience?

Date
Experience (who, what, where, etc.)
Where were you on the comfort zone scale?
What feelings came up for you at this place on the scale?
What reflections, thoughts or insight did you gain from this experience?

Date
Experience (who, what, where, etc.)
Where were you on the comfort zone scale?
What feelings came up for you at this place on the scale?
What reflections, thoughts or insight did you gain from this experience?

Date
Experience (who, what, where, etc.)
Where were you on the comfort zone scale?
What feelings came up for you at this place on the scale?
What reflections, thoughts or insight did you gain from this experience?

Activity Seven: Journaling Culture Shock

Purpose:

This activity will help you better understand, recognize and process the various stages of culture shock. It is an activity that can be done whenever you like and as frequently as you choose.

Introduction:

If you've embarked on a life of adventure (or even just taken a long vacation) you've probably heard of the stages of culture shock. There are a variety of models, but they all go something like this:

Honeymoon Stage: You've just set out on your adventure and everything is wonderful. All of the people you meet are amazing, the food is perfect, and even little mishaps feel like part of the adventure. Things couldn't get any better.

Negotiation Stage: This is the heart of the "shock" in culture shock. At this point, you start to notice that everything isn't actually perfect. You may begin to feel frustration or anxiety. Suddenly you feel like you can't communicate, nothing seems to work the way it should, the people frustrate you and the culture seems backward, strange or unreasonable. Unfortunately, some people get stuck here, but if they can successfully manage this phase things really start to look up.

Adjustment Stage: After a certain amount of time, you begin to feel more at ease in the new culture. You may not understand everything, but you develop a more nuanced understanding of the ins and outs of things. You recognize your own challenges, but stop blaming them on your new culture and begin to see them for what they are – your own process of feeling a part of something different to you.

Mastery Stage: This is the stage at which you feel completely comfortable in your new culture. Most people living or traveling abroad will not get to this phase. Immigrants who live longer term in a new home are much more likely to eventually arrive at this stage. But, this doesn't mean that most expats don't develop certain areas of mastery – particularly in areas of social custom, language and everyday tasks.

Instructions:

This activity can help you better recognize the various stages of culture shock. It serves as a journal for both positive and negative experiences. In the spaces on the next page, you can briefly journal (5-10 sentences) the details of a particular success or setback in your transition. In the column next to the journaling space, take time to think about and then note where you are in the culture shock process and how it might be affecting your experience. Keep in mind you may find you repeat some of the stages. The culture shock process does not necessarily move in a straight line.

It can also be helpful to read back over the experiences as you plan for additional transitions. We learn well by reviewing past successes and failures. There is space here for 12 entries, but of course others can be added on additional sheets of paper or in your own journal.

DATE	EXPERIENCE	CULTURE SHOCK STAGE

DATE	EXPERIENCE	CULTURE SHOCK STAGE

World Tree Coaching
www.worldtreecoaching.com

DATE	EXPERIENCE	CULTURE SHOCK STAGE

World Tree Coaching
www.worldtreecoaching.com

World Tree Coaching

Activity Eight: Balancing You

Purpose:

This exercise will help you identify your strengths and growth areas and then pinpoint specific ways to keep these parts of yourself in balance. This is a great exercise to do at the beginning of a transition, but one you will come back to regularly to rebalance.

Introduction:

It may come as a big shocker, but no one is perfect. If you've taken on a life of international travel, plan to take on such a life or just really like to try new things – there's no doubt you've had someone you know say, "Wow! That's so cool! You're amazing." For the record – you are amazing. But, that doesn't mean you don't find this whole thing incredibly challenging sometimes.

This is because we all have things that push at our weaknesses. Living the expat life can push at those weaknesses even harder. However, by expanding your awareness so that you can play to your strengths, without getting overwhelmed or bogged down in the things you find challenging, you have the power to reveal new and creative ways to handle difficult situations.

Instructions:

1. In the spaces below, list 5 things that come easily to you. These can be skills that are applicable to any area of your life – from the personal to the professional. Then, list 5 things you find challenging – be honest!

I find it easy to:	I find it challenging to:
1.	1.
2.	2.
3.	3.
4.	4.
5.	5.

2. Now, look at the list. Are there any strengths that could complement or address any of the challenges? Don't worry if you can't find a match for each one – there are certainly some that will fit together perfectly. For example, let's say one of your strengths is that you're good at making friends. And, in the other column, perhaps you've listed that you find it challenging to be alone. What a great opportunity to play to your strengths and own up to what makes you feel confident and secure! If you don't like to be alone, but you're great at making friends – you've got the answer to addressing your challenge right in front of you. Yes, that might sound like an easy one, but these are exactly the types of things we overlook when we find ourselves in new and unusual circumstances.

3. Now, using the template below – write some specific strategies to address each of your challenge areas (a total of 8 template spaces are provided). One example is provided.

I find it challenging to _____*be alone*_____, but I find it easy to _____*make new friends*_____. I will use this strength to address this challenge by: (1) _*accepting invitations to do new things*_, (2) _*inviting people over for coffee*_ and (3) _*joining a yoga or Pilates class*_.

I find it challenging to _____, but I find it easy to _____. I will use this strength to address this challenge by: (1) _____,
(2) _____, and
(3) _____.

I find it challenging to _____, but I find it easy to _____. I will use this strength to address this challenge by: (1) _____,
(2) _____, and
(3) _____.

I find it challenging to _____, but I find it easy to _____. I will use this strength to address this challenge by: (1) _____,
(2) _____, and
(3) _____.

I find it challenging to _____, but I find it easy to _____. I will use this strength to address this challenge by: (1) _____,
(2) _____, and
(3) _____.

I find it challenging to _____, but I find it easy to _____. I will use this strength to address this challenge by: (1) _____,
(2) _____, and
(3) _____.

I find it challenging to _____, but I find it easy to _____. I will use this strength to address this challenge by: (1) _____,
(2) _____, and
(3) _____.

I find it challenging to _____, but I find it easy to _____. I will use this strength to address this challenge by: (1) _____,
(2) _____, and
(3) _____.

I find it challenging to _____, but I find it easy to _____. I will use this strength to address this challenge by: (1) _____,
(2) _____, and
(3) _____.

World Tree Coaching

Activity Nine: Community

Purpose:

This activity will help you take stock of your community – including people you never even considered! It will enable you to more clearly see (and remember) that you're not alone. This is a great activity for starting your journey, but you will come back to it often.

Introduction:

For many, the key to surviving in the midst of transition is learning to recognize, develop and trust the community around us. Sometimes this can be easier said than done. When we're experiencing a high degree of change, sometimes it takes significant effort to keep in touch – even with the people that mean the most in our lives. But, that doesn't mean that we don't continue to benefit from all kinds of connection.

Instructions:

1) For each category, name at least 5 people that you know you can count on. Now, that may not mean you can always count on these people for every single thing, but they're the people you know you can count on in some way, no matter what. Do this for each category.

Family	Friends

Colleagues	Acquaintances (This can include people you know via social media, but not face-to-face.)

┌─────────────────────────────┐ ┌─────────────────────────────┐
│ **Helping Professionals** │ │   **Strangers**   │
│ (e.g. doctors, counselors, │ │ (Yes, that's right. E.g. the │
│   HR reps, teachers)   │ │ salesperson you see everyday│
│   │ │   at the bakery or bank) │
└─────────────────────────────┘ └─────────────────────────────┘

2) Step two is a bit more challenging. Generally speaking, people are prone to say, "I've done enough." This can especially be true when we're building a sense of community. It can be easy to tell yourself that you don't want to bother people, that you don't want to put people on the spot or to seem needy. But, sometimes even a little bit of extra effort can enable us to find a stronger sense of community – even with people we already know are our biggest fans. So, with that in mind, look back over the list. Put a symbol (anything that works for you – a check mark, a heart, a star, whatever) next to the people you might be able to get to know better. Then, schedule a time to reach out to that person. For the people you're especially close to that can mean inviting them out for an evening, scheduling a Skype session or sending a nice email. For people you barely know, it can be as simple as a heartfelt, "How's your day?"

3) If you're having trouble thinking of some ways to connect and create, use the space below to do some brainstorming. And remember – you're not bothering people! This is simply an exercise in the law of attraction. You get back what you give out. In this crazy life we all need a sense of community – reach for what you need and in return your community will reach back for you.

┌──┐
│   **IDEAS FOR REACHING OUT FOR COMMUNITY**   │
│   │
│   │
│   │
│   │
└──┘

World Tree Coaching

Activity Ten: Lost and Found

Purpose:

This activity is about looking more closely at the complex person that is You. Here you will have the opportunity to fully let go of the parts of yourself you're fine with giving up, or to bring back into your life the parts of you that you never meant to lose. And, as part of examining that loss, you're also invited in this activity to give yourself credit for new skills you've found – even the ones you never in a million years imagined you'd call your own. While the activity can be done at any time, it is especially useful during times when you feel like you're leaving parts of yourself behind.

Introduction:

Moving around a lot, leaving your home, and trying something new all give you incredible opportunities to find new parts of yourself. But, anyone who's ever taken on a life of adventure readily recognizes that these experiences come with a certain degree of loss.

While most of us probably know these changes are happening within us, we often fail to take the time to examine what we've given up and what new skills or traits we've brought into our lives. When we don't take time for this introspection, we increase our chances of feeling anchorless, lost and alone. We truly lose sense of who we have become during the many transitions we've faced.

Instructions:

1) THE LOST: The following activity can be completed in the spaces provided, but feel free to add additional spaces on your own paper, in a journal, etc.

    In the chart, write a brief reflection on a part of yourself you have lost. This can be a skill, a dream, a stubborn personality trait (good riddance to that one?), or even a relationship that time and space has strained.

    Then, in the "So now what?" section, decide what you want to do about that loss. Is this part of your life worth getting back? Is it perhaps better to leave it behind? Would you bring it back with some caveats? Make a decision about it.

    Finally, in the last section (Moving On...) jot down a few ideas for how you might follow through with your plan. Now, of course, bringing back lost parts of you life is much more challenging than just making a list, but the goal here is brainstorming. Put this loss back on your radar for a bit. If it's something you want to get back into your life – how might you go about that? If it's something you're happy to have left behind, how will you make sure it stays in the past? What space will you give yourself to celebrate its passing? Give yourself complete freedom here to do what feels right to you. Then, challenge yourself to follow through with your plans in a way that makes sense for you.

LOST
SO NOW WHAT?
MOVING ON...

LOST
SO NOW WHAT?
MOVING ON...

LOST
SO NOW WHAT?
MOVING ON...

LOST
SO NOW WHAT?
MOVING ON…

2) THE FOUND: In the spaces below, take time to look at the new things that have come up in your life. The first step is simply identifying them. Sometimes they sneak up on us. Think of all of the things you never would have imagined you're able to do! Write them down.

Then, as with the losses, decide whether these new parts of you are worth keeping around. Are they perfect for your lifestyle? Are there parts that are benefitting you and other aspects of them that you'd be happy to leave behind?

Finally, create some ideas for how to nurture these new traits into fully become part of you, or decide how you might let them go. As before, this is an idea-generating exercise – where you choose to go with your ideas is up to you.

FOUND
SO NOW WHAT?
MOVING ON…

FOUND
SO NOW WHAT?
MOVING ON…

FOUND
SO NOW WHAT?
MOVING ON…

FOUND
SO NOW WHAT?
MOVING ON…

World Tree Coaching
www.worldtreecoaching.com

Activity Eleven: Taking Credit for New Skills

Purpose:

This exercise will help you keep track of and take credit for the new skills and talents you gain during your life of international adventure. It's another great anytime exercise.

Introduction:

When you spend a lot of time transitioning, it can be easy to get down on yourself. Often we hold ourselves to such a ridiculously high standard that we completely fail to take note of all of the amazing skills we're learning and only focus on our failures.

Instructions:

Use this list to remind yourself of all of the new things you've learned on your journey (or journeys). Remember that you can put anything on this list – no matter how small. Don't forget things like learning how to bargain at a market, to drive with a completely different set of traffic rules (or no traffic rules at all!), to convert currency at a rapid, brain-busting pace or to make metric-to-standard measurement conversions…or vice versa. These are skills, and before you embarked on this path you didn't have them. Take credit, add things as they come along and read this list when you're sitting in self-judgment. Hold your head up! Shine!

The new skills you gain start piling up fast! There is space here for 50 items. Start the list off with a few things you already know how to do. Then, fill the rest up with new skills as you acquire them.

50 Things I Can Do Now (That I Had Never Done Before)
1.
2.
3.
4.
5.
6.
7.
8.

9.
10.
11.
12.
13.
14.
15.
16.
17.
18.
19.
20.
21.
22.
23.
24.
25.
26.
27.
28.
29.

30.
31.
32.
33.
34.
35.
36.
37.
38.
39.
40.
41.
42.
43.
44.
45.
46.
47.
48.
49.
50.

Activity Twelve: Your Life Story

Purpose:

This exercise will help you reclaim the narrative of your life. It is designed to provide insights into past successes and challenges. While it can be done at any time, it is especially helpful when you're feeling like things are not within your control.

Introduction:

The expat experience is often a long and extended exercise in learning about control. You have to be constantly on top of every single detail of your life. The passports, the packing, the flights, the bills, the kids, the schools, require endless structuring, confirming and double-checking. And, when all of that's said and done, something (something outside your control) invariably comes along and makes short work of your dedicated planning.

It's possible that life will always feel like you're walking a tightrope between order and chaos, but you have the ability to choose how you approach that journey. The first step in that process is looking back at the choices that have brought you to where you are now. By doing this, in your own words and from your own perspective, you have the opportunity to see not only when you were truly in control, but how you handled the inevitable and unexpected disruptions.

Instructions:

In this exercise you will write your life story. That's it. Nothing fancy. Write in any style you desire and be as creative as you want to. Detail any important time periods, accomplishments and highlights of your life. Use the space provided, or type it, print and tape it here, or use a journal. After you've written it, take time to look back over all of the awesome things you've done, the incredible challenges you've faced, the difficult times when you've come out on top and the times when you really did reach the bottom. Claim this story for yourself. It's yours. Choose it. It's beautiful and it's all your own.

_____
_____
_____
_____
_____
_____
_____
_____
_____
_____
_____
_____
_____
_____
_____
_____
_____
_____
_____

World Tree Coaching
www.worldtreecoaching.com

Activity Thirteen: The Space Box

Purpose:

This activity is about creating space you can take with you. It's a simple exercise that can be done at any time before, during or after transition. It is really a start whenever, do whenever, keep forever project.

Introduction:

For those of us who live a mobile lifestyle, it can be very challenging to create space – space to put our stuff, space to be ourselves, space for our memories and space for our hopes of things to come. We often end up bottling them up inside us and, really, sometimes there's no better place than the heart to carry the things that can easily be transported. But at the same time, when you lack a permanent home, it can be helpful to maintain something concrete and physical. That's where the Space Box comes in.

Supplies:

A box – preferably a small one. It doesn't have to be anything fancy, but you will want to find something that you're comfortable having out and present, so visually appealing to you is important.

Trinkets – one or two things of personal significance. The longer you use the box, the more things you'll likely have.

What to Do:

Find a place that you love – a place with which you have positive or important memories. Sit or stand comfortably in that place. Open the box. Close your eyes and be present with whatever your senses are telling you – the sounds, the smells, the air, the emotions and thoughts that come up for you. Now, imagine all of those energies joining together and visualize them being collected in the box – your space, coming together for you, in this little space. And then close the box. When you arrive wherever you're going – open the box. Do the ritual in reverse. Acknowledge the space from the place (or places) you came from accompanying you to your new home. Leave the box open – on your dresser, your desk, your nightstand. See it and remember that where you were before is a part of where you are now.

You can repeat this process everywhere you go – leaving and collecting space and arriving and releasing space. It's a tiny (and highly portable) reminder that you're always, always at home.

Activity Fourteen: Life's Little Go-Bag

Purpose:

This activity will help you focus on what matters most. It's an exercise in gratitude. It can be done at anytime, but you will especially appreciate the results if you do it at a time when you're feeling especially unthankful. After completing it, look back on it regularly for its fantastic reminders.

Introduction:

Every expat has (or probably should have...or has been told they should have) a go-bag. The bag of things you grab when the...well...you know what...hits the fan. Where you're living, this might be a coup d'état or an earthquake, but it could even be the sudden death or illness of someone with you abroad or someone back home. The bottom line is, it's a bag of things you can't live without.

And yet, we all know that at the end of the day, the things in that bag are replaceable. But what's not replaceable? Your values? Your sense of self worth? Your health? The lives of the people you love most?

Instructions:

In this activity you're invited to make a go-bag of what matters most. Get creative. Draw, color, label, or use photos. Fill up the suitcase below with images of gratitude of the things that mean the most. Leave the image here in this book or place it somewhere as a reminder. Or complete the entire activity in your journal or on a separate piece of paper.

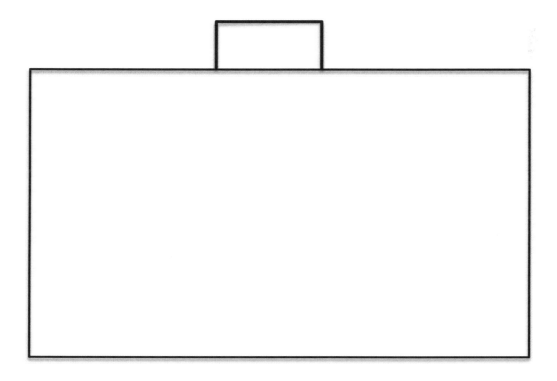

Activity Fifteen: 20 Questions for Getting Unstuck

Purpose:

This activity is designed to help you gain insight and clarity. You can do it at any time – all at once, or one question at a time.

Introduction:

Let's face it – sometimes you just feel stuck. Everyday you're dealing with really big decisions. And, these decisions don't just affect you. They affect your family, your friends and every single aspect of your lifestyle – from health insurance to education.

When we're contemplating what's next, it can be really easy to feel overwhelmed. It can be difficult to see things clearly. At some point we have to begin to face the questions that we've always avoided asking. The thing about those of us who like to see the world is that we often suffer from a kind of "grass is always greener" sort of mentality. We may love what we're doing, but can't shake the nagging feeling that maybe there's something better out there. Well, maybe there is…or maybe not. But, before you start throwing out your suitcases or tearing up your passports, you owe it to yourself to really look at what's going on.

Instructions:

This exercise is an anytime exercise. It's simply a list of questions to ask yourself – all at once or periodically one-by-one. Approach the list however you see fit. You can make a schedule for yourself (for example, one question per week until they're all answered) or just pick up the list when you're feeling especially unsure. Use the spaces provided, your own paper, or a journal. The key is to be honest. Feel free to let your mind wander. Use this like kindling in a fire and then just give yourself time to see where it takes you.

1. What do I really, really, really, really want?

2. Of all the things I do, what do I enjoy doing most?

3. What am I afraid of?

4. What part of myself am I working hardest to hide from others?

5. What am I both good at <u>and</u> enjoy doing?

6. What am I good at, but <u>don't</u> enjoy doing?

7. Who are the 5 people in my life that most inspire me? Why?

8. What are 3 times in my life when I was faced with a decision and I made the right choice for me at that time?

9. Who am I judging? What does it say about me that I'm holding that judgment?

10. What aspect of my life gives me the greatest sense of purpose?

11. Who are the people in my life with whom I feel the most "me?"

12. What are 3 things in my life that I am tolerating?

13. Where do I want to go that I've never been?

14. What do I want to say that I've never said?

15. Who in my life loves me most of all?

16. What emotions or feelings freak me out?

17. What would I prefer to do less of?

18. What would I prefer to do more of?

19. When do I feel closest to God? (God, as you define it – whatever draws you closer to your spiritual center)

20. If tomorrow were my last day, what would I let go of?

Activity Sixteen: Bad Day Permission Slip

Purpose:

This activity gives you the opportunity to prepare in advance to cut yourself some slack. It's perfect for planning ahead for bad days...because they will definitely happen.

Introduction:

Even if you really, really love a life of adventure, at some point you're going to have a bad day. The thing is, we expats like to believe we're made of steel. Now, while it's true we are capable of anything (seriously, Anything!), some days we just get slammed with the sense that this is all a bit too much to handle.

Instructions:

You are amazing! You are incredibly smart, talented, funny and someone's very best friend in the whole world. You owe it to yourself to do (on the really hard days) what you need to do to feel better. You can take care of yourself. Start your list here and refer back to it whenever you need to. Be bold – let the laundry sit an extra day, turn in a project a day late, have a glass of wine and a movie (even if you've got bills to pay)...the list is endless...and you're worth it!

On a bad day, I give myself permission to:

Activity Seventeen: Your Life Vision

Purpose:

The following exercise is designed to help you begin the process of re-envisioning your life. If your life is exactly as you want it, then the exercise will help you to clarify your vision. This can really be done whenever, but it works especially well as a planner when you're in a relatively stable place knowing that a transition is on the horizon.

Introduction:

It's common in life to have the moment when you say, "This is it. Here I am. This is me." Author and blogger Gretchen Rubin calls this the *Beautiful House Moment*. As in, "This is not my beautiful house," from the Talking Heads song "Once in A Lifetime." The song hits upon that moment when you realize that maybe things aren't exactly as you thought they would be…or maybe they are. But, at any rate, you look around you and you wonder how you came to be so firmly and irreversibly planted exactly where you are.

There's something to be said for accepting life as it is – the ups, the downs and all the in-betweens. I believe, even in difficulty, we can learn from our ability to see things as they are and act from *that* place rather than from a place of misconception, mistrust, anxiety or fear. But, *to act* is the key here. If things don't look the way you want, the way you always dreamed they would, or the way you truly hoped they would be, why not make a change?

Instructions:

Use the blanks below to describe your life exactly as you would like it to be. This should be an accurate reflection of your vision of your ideal life. After completing the sentences, organize what you have re-envisioned into a paragraph. This paragraph will serve as your Life Vision Statement. Use it as a reminder of the direction in which you're going, your values and your dreams.

1. In my family life I am committed to:

2. I develop my professional self (or my mind) by:

3. For recreation and fun I enjoy:

4. My home environment is:

5. My retirement lifestyle looks like:

6. My hobbies, passions, creative pursuits and interests are:

7. I maintain my health by:

MY LIFE VISION STATEMENT

Using the information you have gathered about yourself in the above worksheet, write your personal vision in paragraph form.

_____
_____
_____
_____
_____
_____
_____
_____
_____
_____
_____
_____
_____
_____
_____
_____
_____
_____
_____
_____
_____

World Tree Coaching
www.worldtreecoaching.com

Activity Eighteen: Dressing for What's Next

Purpose:

This exercise can help you examine personal changes you've experienced and the ways in which those experiences have become a part of you. It's ideal for preparing for re-entry into your home culture or for periods of transition.

Introduction:

When we transition a lot we collect memories, experiences and new parts of our personalities like coats and gloves and scarves on a snowy day. Sometimes we wear all of the layers. Then, when the setting changes, we just wear bits and pieces. We're constantly making adjustments based on what we find in the world around us.

There are times when this experience is most acute. Transition back to our home culture can be a time when we almost fear wearing the layers of experience we've acquired. What once felt like normal now seems strange. We wear our new vocabulary, our new sense of personal space, our new customs and even our new skills shyly. We worry about standing out for the new parts of ourselves that have come to feel so natural.

Instructions:

In this activity, you will prepare a visual reminder of the different layers you wear. Practice telling yourself that these parts of you are not for hiding, but new, fantastic and complicated patterns of the coat, the scarf and the gloves that make up who you are. Let your creativity flow in this exercise. Use words, pictures, magazine clippings, etc. to create an image of yourself (stick figures are fine!) on the next page with all of the new words, customs, habits and traditions that you've acquired. If you want, cut it out and hang it up somewhere as a visual reminder to wear your new layers with confidence.

Activity Nineteen: On Thoughts and Emotions

Purpose:

This exercise will help you identify and process the many thoughts and feelings that come up during transition and throughout the stages of culture shock.

Introduction:

Does this scenario sound familiar? You're out for a walk (or up late at night, or cooking dinner, or driving to work) and a million and one thoughts are racing through your mind. This isn't unique to expats, but for expats it includes the additional mental clutter that is passports and plane tickets and moving boxes and school changes and time changes and…well, you know how it goes.

The challenge with all of this mental processing (besides the fact that it's exhausting) is that it either extends or crowds out what is really happening emotionally. Here's an example:

Let's say you find out that your home's Internet access will be down for three days. You've just moved and you're missing your best friend terribly. When you hear the Internet will be down and you'll miss a Skype session you had scheduled with her, you feel sad. Suddenly, your brain kicks into gear – "This is crazy! How can the Internet be down for three days! Someone is not doing his job! This is because we've just moved here! They don't care about us new people!" You might fire off a quick (and maybe regrettable) email to whomever you think may be responsible. You might yell at your kids. Perhaps you complain openly and negatively to someone in your spouse's office – hoping your annoyance will be conveyed onward.

So there are two things working here. On the one hand, you're extending the original emotion of sadness – drawing it out, perhaps even turning it into anger, resentment, frustration, etc. You've made it bigger and more painful than it may have been. On the other hand, the emotion (and the time to really sit with it) is being crowded out in your mind and heart by all of the thoughts you have around it. And, these two aspects work in conjunction – feeding each other. The more you think about how frustrated you are, the more upset you become. The more upset you become, the more likely your brain is to go into overdrive looking for answers. And, when we are in a vulnerable position (like living or working outside our home culture), it's even easier to let our emotions and then our thoughts overtake us.

But, there's hope. This exercise will help you create a framework for identifying thoughts versus emotions and then give you a strategy for dealing with them in the moment. It is based in the concepts of mindfulness meditation. You can find great information on mindfulness meditation on the web and in print. If you like this exercise, consider doing some Internet searching to learn more about these ideas and the practice of mindfulness meditation.

Instructions:

1) In this first step, you will spend some time getting honest with your emotions. Of course, on a daily basis any one person can feel a whole range of emotions so this list may not necessarily be exhaustive. However, in the spaces below, choose 5-10 emotions that you feel are more or less everyday feelings for you. Then, to the right describe how those emotions usually feel for you physically (in other words, what signs is your body giving you that these emotions are present). It may or may not come easily to describe the physical sensation of the emotions. It may be necessary to take some time noticing the emotions when they're happening before trying to tackle the list. List both "positive" and "negative" emotions. Two examples are provided.

Emotion	Description
Happiness	I feel butterflies in my stomach. My feet move like they want to dance. My face naturally breaks into a smile.
Frustration	I grind my teeth. Sometimes I feel like it's difficult to hold back tears. I get tense in my neck and shoulders.

World Tree Coaching
www.worldtreecoaching.com

2) The next step in this activity is to begin to label the parts of your personality that are driven by thoughts. Think of these parts of yourself as mini-professionals living inside you. There's the professional worrier, the fixer, the planner, the escape artist, etc. etc. You'll notice these parts of you when you're doing lots and lots of thinking. In the spaces below, think of 4-5 prominent parts of your personality and give them names. You can get really creative on this. It's okay to make up brand new words – your own special part of you. Then, in the spaces to the right, list 2-3 typical or recent thoughts that are representative of that part of yourself. A couple of examples are provided.

The Mini-Professional	Example Thoughts
The Worrier	"The healthcare in our new country might be really lacking. What if the kids get sick? Will we have access to doctors?" "My wife is traveling for 2 weeks. What if something happens to her? How will I be able to care for the children alone?"
The Judge	"These people who have just moved here don't understand anything about this country. Isn't this common sense!?" "No one ever comes to visit us here! If my family lived abroad, I would always make the effort. It's like they don't even care."

3) Congratulations! Step 1 and Step 2 are probably the most challenging parts of this exercise. It can be difficult to distinguish thoughts from feelings – the two are so intertwined. But, what you have now done is created (first) a framework for identifying emotions when they crop up and (second) categories into which you can place all of those thoughts that can overtake your mental space.

Completing the first two parts of this exercise has likely kicked off some personal growth already. Oftentimes, we're not even aware of what is going on in our hearts and our minds. But, the growth does not have to stop there.

The next step in this process is to begin to cultivate more regular awareness around these emotions and thoughts when they're happening. In many ways, simply acknowledging and using the labels and categories you've created provides you with an incredible opportunity for getting more in tune with your own perceptions and experience. When you say to yourself "I'm feeling really sad. My stomach is in knots and I want to cry. And, now I'm starting to worry that my relationships with my friends back home are going to start to suffer because of the distance between us. And now I'm worrying about how this lifestyle affects my children," you're connecting directly with (1) the real emotion as it is happening and (2) the thought patterns that come from and then reinforce that emotion.

Because this exercise represents ongoing work, the process for making it work for you in the long-term is up to you. For Step 3, choose one of the suggested activities below and try it out. Give yourself a time frame for putting the activity into place. Monitor not only your progress with the activity itself, but also any growth or insight you have around your thoughts and emotions, and how they play out in your daily life (a journal can be great for this). Be flexible – if one of the suggested activities doesn't work for you, try something else. Be creative – give yourself the space to modify the activity if you feel like something else would work better. Be patient and forgiving – the activity you're undertaking may represent a huge stretch for you, so it's really okay if some days (or even most days) things don't go exactly as you had hoped.

Suggestions for cultivating awareness for every day:

(1) Find a time to practice some form of daily meditation. Five, ten or fifteen minutes is fine. The goal here is to find a quiet place, where you won't be interrupted. When there, simply spend some time noticing and naming the thoughts and emotions that arise. As you bring this in to your life, you may find that you would prefer to do a longer practice – that's fine too.

(2) Name that feeling! Name that mini-professional at work in your brain! This is probably one of the least intrusive activities to try because you can really do it any time and any where with very little change in your schedule. The biggest challenge is remembering to do it. Practice this activity by naming (out loud or to yourself) which emotions and thoughts patterns are present in a given situation. For example, if you find yourself walking into work feeling tense, with butterflies in your stomach – you might say in your head, "anxious." You might also notice that you're calculating costs for your next move, so you might name the mini-professional – "that's The Planner in me." If you can find times to do this here and there, you'll notice you get better at it and that with time you will become more and more aware of your daily emotional and cognitive habits.

(3) Do some things, each day, on purpose. This is about cutting out some of your multi-tasking so that you can create a greater awareness of what's happening in the moment. It doesn't just mean taking time to stop checking your email – while cooking dinner and helping your daughter practice her spelling words – it means taking time to do *one thing* and to have all of your emotional and mental energy focused just on that one thing. Take brushing your teeth for example. Instead of simply brushing away, take time to notice how you're feeling emotionally. Stressed because you're late for work? Happy because the day is winding down and you're looking forward to getting in bed with a good book? Also look at what thoughts are running through your head and acknowledge which mini-professional is running the show. Then, take time to greet and name these thoughts and feelings (just a simple, "Yes, hello there anxiety.") and then redirect your energy fully back to the task at hand, paying full attention to the experience of that task.

(4) Make some introductions! In all situations, we benefit from making a human connection. While it can be difficult to open up to people, more often than not, when we do we find that we face common emotions, thoughts and challenges. So, for this activity, introduce some of the emotions or mini-professionals you've become acquainted with in this exercise to a friend. What does that mean exactly? This is about taking time to show your true and authentic self to those around you – especially the people that matter most. That doesn't, of course, mean sharing in ways in which you're not comfortable, but it can mean sharing in a way that is slightly outside of the norm for you. So, for example, let's say you're struggling with stress over your next move, but your inclination is to keep that discomfort to yourself. Instead of holding all of this in, tell a friend, your spouse/partner or family member. And, this is true for sharing your mini-professionals as well. It's okay to say things like, "The micro-manager in me is really needing to have this project finished. Even though this is a holiday, I'm going to take 30 minutes to put in a little bit of work." When you own up to these parts of yourself, you're moving towards freeing yourself from the burden of solo mental struggle and emotional isolation, and you'll find this skill becoming a major asset in all aspects of your life.

Activity Twenty: The Goodbye Checklist

Purpose:

This exercise will help you pinpoint the things, people, places or experiences that you're committed to really taking time to say goodbye to. It's perfect for preparing for departure.

Introduction:

There's simply no denying it – this lifestyle is full (as in spilling over completely) with goodbyes. It is part and parcel of the package that is a life of international adventure.

And, the time is going to come where you know you need to start saying goodbye. It's typical to feel overwhelmed at this stage. Many people simply get a case of *senioritis* and distance themselves emotionally from what's happening. There are some benefits to this and it is a natural reaction, but we can also plan for our goodbyes in a way that leaves us with fewer regrets and better closure so that we can move on more fully to the next phase.

Instructions:

In the spaces provided, take time to plan your goodbyes. As with the Hello Checklist, the opportunities and must-dos have the potential to become overwhelming, but in taking time to note the things that are most important, you give yourself permission to make time for only the ones that really matter to you. Add additional spaces as needed.

My Must Dos	Done
Ex. Mindfully buy mangos one last time from the man on the corner. Look him in the eye and say, "Thank you."	✓

World Tree Coaching
www.worldtreecoaching.com

Made in the USA
Middletown, DE
27 February 2015